Contents

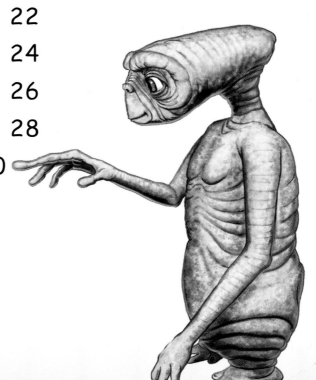

The Earth in Space

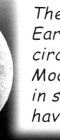

The Earth is one of nine round worlds, called planets, that move around the Sun. The Sun is a star, one of millions in the sky. No other star is as close to us, or as bright, as the Sun. From E.T.'s spacecraft, our Earth looks like a spinning blue ball.

Oceans make the Earth look blue. Other planets are too hot or cold to have oceans.

The Moon circles the Earth as the Earth circles the Sun. The Moon is the only object in space that humans have visited.

How the Earth formed

Scientists think the Sun and planets formed from a cloud of space dust and gas. About 4,600 million years ago, gravity pulled the cloud together, squeezing it into the giant, hot Sun and cooler planets.

E.T.™
THE EXTRA-TERRESTRIAL
DISCOVERS
Planet Earth

Simon Smiley

KINGFISHER/UNIVERSAL
Kingfisher Publications Plc
New Penderel House
283-288 High Holborn
London WC1V 7HZ
www.kingfisherpub.com

First published by Kingfisher Publications Plc in 2002

10 9 8 7 6 5 4 3 2 1

1TR/1201/TWP/MAR(MAR)/130SINAR

ISBN 0 7534 0734 5

Printed in Singapore

Author: Simon Smiley
Project Manager: Belinda Weber
Editor: Christine Hatt
Art Editor: Eljay Yildirim
Designer: Andrew Nash
DTP Manager: Nicky Studdart
Production Controller: Debbie Otter,
Kelly Johnson

Day and night

The Earth makes a complete turn once a day. Dawn comes in the places where the Earth is turning to face the Sun. Half a turn later, night falls in the same places as they move into the Earth's shadow again.

Gravity

An invisible force called gravity pulls heavy objects towards each other. In space, gravity keeps the planets circling the Sun. The same force pulls things on the Earth towards its centre, giving them weight. If there were no gravity, people would float around in the air.

5

Earth's Crusty Shell

The outside of our planet is a hard, cold crust. The crust floats on hot, melted rock. At the centre of the Earth is a big metal ball. The Earth's crust seems very solid to you and me, but E.T.'s sensitive feet tell him the ground is slowly moving.

Supercontinent

Millions of years ago, all the land on the Earth was one huge supercontinent. Slowly, it broke up and the pieces drifted apart to form Africa, Asia, Europe and the Americas. You can see from their shape that the continents used to fit together like a jigsaw puzzle.

PHONE HOME FACTS

The Earth's plates move apart under the oceans. Near the gaps between them, there are holes in the seabed. Hot sea water full of minerals pours out of them like smoke.

You could not eat your lunch off the rocky plates of the Earth's crust. The smallest is 10 million times bigger than a dinner plate!

Drifting lands

The Earth's crust is split into huge pieces called plates. There are seven large plates and some small ones. The plates are always moving against each other and where they meet they can cause mountains and valleys to form or disturbances, such as earthquakes.

PLATE EDGES

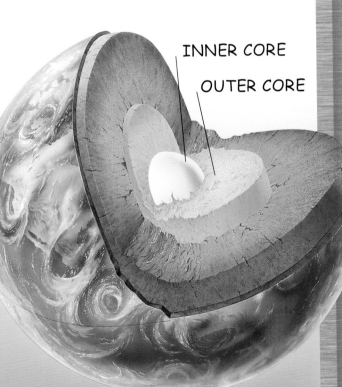

INNER CORE

OUTER CORE

Scientists cannot visit the centre of the Earth, called the core. But echoes from earthquakes give them clues about what is inside our planet. The inner core is made of solid iron. The outer core is made of liquid iron.

INFORMATION OVERLOAD!

E.T. has collected so many fascinating facts that he must send them back to his planet to be analysed.

The plates of the Earth's crust move very slowly. Europe and the Americas are drifting apart about two-and-a-half centimetres each year.

In places, the Earth's crust is only six kilometres thick. A fast lift could travel through it in just 10 minutes.

The temperature of the Earth's inner core is 5,700°C. That is 20 times hotter than the hottest kitchen oven.

Rocks and Minerals

Rocks are rough. Rocks are hard. Rocks are solid. The Earth's crust is made of them, but E.T. knows they do not provide just a firm base for roads and houses. From them, people can also dig up special stones called minerals and the fuels coal, gas and oil.

BASALT

The past preserved

Rocks made from mud contain preserved animal and plant remains called fossils. These tell us how life on the Earth began. Fossil fuels – coal, oil and gas – are the remains of forests that grew 300 million years ago.

How rocks formed

The Earth's rocks formed in three main ways. Melted material that flowed up from below the crust formed fiery rocks, such as basalt. When fiery rocks crumbled, their remains formed muddy layers. These slowly hardened to form a second type of rocks, such as sandstone. Heat and pressure changed these rocks into a third type. They include quartz.

SANDSTONE

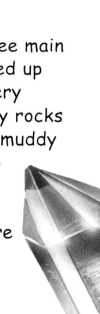

QUARTZ

TURQUOISE

GARNET

AMETHYST

AQUAMARINE

DIAMOND

EMERALD

Crystals and gems

Pure minerals sometimes form crystals in the rocks. Crystals are glassy shapes with sharp angles, often in bright colours. Gems such as diamonds and emeralds are rare crystals. People cut and polish them to make them sparkle, then use them for jewellery.

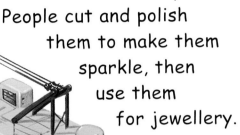

We dig mines and quarries to find minerals. Most minerals are not pure enough to use at once. To make iron or gold, machines must crush the rocks that miners dig up, then take out the metals.

EARTH ALERT!

Burning fossil fuels such as coal and oil releases a gas that traps the Sun's heat. If we do not start to use different fuels, the Earth's climate will warm up faster and faster, bringing storms, floods and drought.

INFORMATION OVERLOAD!

E.T. has collected so many fascinating facts that he must send them back to his planet to be analysed.

Just one mineral – silica – makes up more than half of the Earth's crust. Silica has many forms. Amethyst, for example, is a type of silica.

There is not much gold in a gold mine. To make enough metal for a wedding ring, machines must crush and process rock weighing as much as a small car.

Diamonds are the hardest natural minerals. This is why they are used to make dentists' drills for cutting into teeth, and industrial drills for cutting into rock.

Earth's Bubble of Life

The bubble of air around the Earth is called the atmosphere. It provides the oxygen and water that humans and E.T. need to live. It also protects us from harmful space rays!

Invisible gas balloon

The atmosphere is a mix of invisible gases that circle the Earth like a balloon. About one-fifth is oxygen, most of the rest is a gas called nitrogen. Plants on the Earth make the oxygen and release it into the atmosphere.

EARTH ALERT!
A layer of ozone gas in the atmosphere helps to keep out harmful rays from the Sun. They cause skin cancer. Chemicals called CFCs in fridges and spray cans have made a hole in the ozone layer.

SPACE BEGINS HERE

Changing atmosphere

Gravity stops the atmosphere from floating away. It pulls hardest near to the Earth's surface, so that is where most of the atmosphere is. The higher up you go, the less air the atmosphere contains. Space begins about 160 kilometres up, where the atmosphere ends.

The atmosphere has four main layers. All weather happens in the lowest layer.

WINTER
SNOWFLAKES

Changing seasons

In many places, each season brings different weather. Seasons happen because the Earth leans over as it circles the Sun. When the top half is nearer the Sun, it is summer there and winter in the lower half. Six months later, the lower half is nearer, so it is summer there and winter in the top half.

SPRING
FLOWERS

SUMMER MEADOW

AUTUMN
LEAVES

Windy weather

The Sun's warmth heats air, and the hot air rises. As it rises, it sucks in more air as wind to fill the space left. The wind stirs up the lowest, dampest part of the atmosphere. This moves heat and wet clouds around the world, changing the weather.

Violent Earth

Under E.T.'s feet, violent forces are at work! Volcanoes spurt red-hot, liquid rock called lava high into the air. Earthquakes shake the ground as if it were jelly. Giant waves smash against the coasts.

When lava comes to the surface of a volcano, we say the volcano is erupting.

Shaky ground

Movement in the Earth's crust causes earthquakes. The plates that make up the crust slide over each other, pull apart or grind together. This builds up pressure in rocks on either side of the cracks. When enough pressure has built up, the rocks jerk and an earthquake happens.

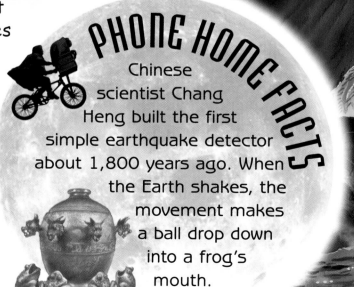

PHONE HOME FACTS

Chinese scientist Chang Heng built the first simple earthquake detector about 1,800 years ago. When the Earth shakes, the movement makes a ball drop down into a frog's mouth.

Fire mountains

Volcanoes form where cracks in the Earth's crust let lava erupt on to the surface. Volcanoes can also throw out ash and poisonous clouds of burning gas. The same thing happens on a much smaller scale when you open a fizzy drink. By taking off the top, you release the pressure and the liquid inside 'erupts'.

Undersea earthquakes shake the ocean floor. The shock makes a tsunami — a strong water ripple that turns into waves. When the waves reach shallow water, they slow and swell, growing as big as skyscrapers. As they crash ashore, they destroy everything.

INFORMATION OVERLOAD!

E.T. has collected so many fascinating facts that he must send them back to his planet to be analysed.

Geologists measure earthquakes on the Richter scale. A quake that scores one is slight. The worst quakes score nine and are 100 million times stronger.

Volcanoes can appear without warning. The volcano Paricutín appeared in Mexico in 1943. Within a day, it was eight metres high. By 1944, it was 325 metres high.

A tsunami that hit the coast of Japan 300 years ago killed at least 100,000 people.

Mountains and Valleys

You need a neck as bendy as E.T.'s to get a good look at mountains! They tower so high that people often cannot see the tops. Mountains grow this big because forces squeeze and crease the Earth's crust upwards all the time.

In dry regions, the wind works like sandpaper. The sand and grit that the wind carries wear away at the rock, smoothing its surface, and changing its shape.

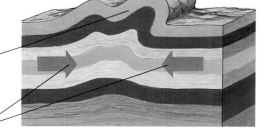

MOUNTAIN RANGE RISES UP

MOVING PLATES SQUEEZE LAND

What makes mountains?

When the plates of the Earth's crust crunch together, land rises up. It creases like a cloth sliding on a table. The creases form mountain ranges. These are long lines of peaks that stretch across continents. The pressure can also force blocks of rock downwards, making deep rift valleys.

Mountain ranges

Mountains are usually crowded together in large groups called ranges. The Rockies range rises on the west edge of North America, and the Andes range on the west edge of South America. The Himalayas, the world's highest range, is in Southern Asia. Europe's mountain range is called the Alps.

The world's highest mountain is Everest, in the Himalayas. It is 8,848 metres high and stands on the border between India and Tibet.

What destroys mountains?

Weather and water destroy mountains. Rain dissolves soft rock, forming caves. Even hard rock shatters when rain gets into cracks and freezes. Broken rock moves downhill in rivers and landslides. The Colorado River carved the USA's huge Grand Canyon out of the rock over millions of years.

INFORMATION OVERLOAD!

E.T. has collected so many fascinating facts that he must send them back to his planet to be analysed.

The tallest mountains are the youngest. The Himalayas reached their record height 1.5 million years ago. The Andes are 40 times older.

East Africa's Great Rift Valley formed when a block of land dropped down between two cracks in the Earth's surface. The Valley is 6,400 kilometres long and up to 2,700 metres deep.

The Andes is the world's longest mountain range. It stretches 7,600 kilometres down South America, from the Caribbean Sea in the north to the tail of Chile in the south.

Cold Lands

If the Earth's oceans were a giant cold drink, the Arctic would be the ice cubes. E.T. has learned that to match this frosty cap in the north, the Earth has another in the south. There, the ice covers a vast continent called Antarctica.

Polar bears live on the edges of the Arctic ice-cap, and swim in the chilly waters of the Arctic Ocean. There they look for fish and seals to eat.

North and South

The Arctic ice-cap, at the top of the Earth, is frozen sea water three to four metres thick. Its centre is the North Pole, an imaginary spot around which the Earth spins. Antarctica's land lies under 2,000-metre thick ice. Its centre is the South Pole, our planet's other turning point.

EARTH ALERT!
The Earth's climate is warming, making both glaciers and sea ice melt. Soon our planet may have an ice-cap only in the south.

Ice that moves

Ice rivers called glaciers slide slowly from snow-covered mountains. The ice scrapes each valley it slides down into a shape like the letter U. When glaciers reach the sea, huge chunks break off to form floating icebergs.

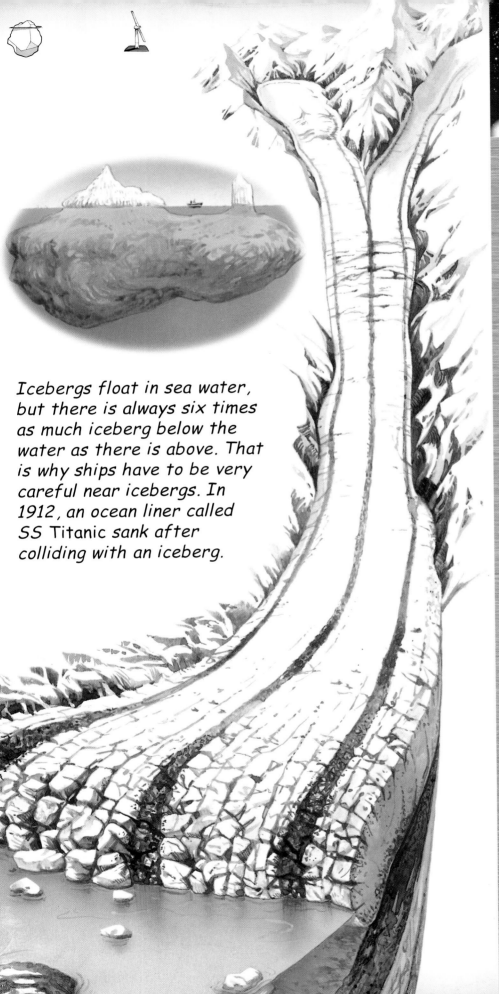

Icebergs float in sea water, but there is always six times as much iceberg below the water as there is above. That is why ships have to be very careful near icebergs. In 1912, an ocean liner called SS Titanic sank after colliding with an iceberg.

INFORMATION OVERLOAD!

E.T. has collected so many fascinating facts that he must send them back to his planet to be analysed.

Three-quarters of the Earth's fresh water is frozen into glaciers and the two ice-caps.

The temperature in Antarctica once fell to -89.2°C. This was cold enough to break most thermometers.

If all the ice in Antarctica were spread evenly over the Earth's continents, it would make a layer as tall as a 14-storey office block.

Seas and Oceans

E.T. has discovered that the Earth is a very soggy planet. Only one-quarter of its surface is dry land. The rest is covered by the salty water of seas and oceans. Just one ocean – the Pacific – covers one-third of the world.

Sea water is salty because rivers dissolve salt from the land, then carry it to the sea. More salt comes from rocks on the seabed. There is about a teaspoonful of salt in every tumblerful of sea water. So don't drink it!

How deep is the sea?

Seas and oceans fill vast basins – low areas – in the Earth's crust. Most of the oceans are about four kilometres deep.

Tides and coasts

The gravity of the Moon and the Sun pulls on the seas and oceans, making the water level rise and fall twice a day. These changes in level are called tides. Wind blowing over the ocean surface causes waves. They tear at rock on the coasts, cutting cliffs, caves and bays. The sea grinds the rock into pebbles and sand, then washes them ashore to form beaches.

Coral islands and reefs

In warm waters, groups of tiny creatures grow on rocks close to the surface. When they die, their tubelike skeletons form stony coral. Enough coral can grow to make an island or reef. A reef is a coral ridge that is separated from the shore by water.

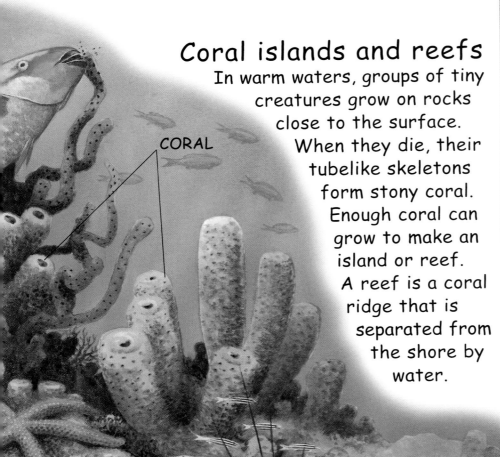

CORAL

Rivers and Wetlands

As they snake down towards the sea, rivers shape the Earth. They carve out deep canyons. They cut winding valleys. They fill lakes and swamps. And they thunder over high rocks as waterfalls. E.T. loves to stand in the cooling spray.

Round and round

The Earth's water goes round and round. Clouds bring rain to the land, then the rain drains into rivers. The rivers flow to the sea. When the Sun heats the sea, the water evaporates. This means it turns into a fine mist. The mist then forms clouds and the water starts to go round again.

Where do rivers come from?

When it rains, the water soaks down into the land until it reaches hard rock. Then the water starts to flow sideways instead. When it reaches the surface again, it forms a spring. Many rivers begin at springs. Others start where rainwater collects in a lake or swamp.

Squelchy swamps

Wetlands are a mixture of water and dry land. You can find wetlands such as swamps and marshes on river banks. They also form where land slopes too gently for water to drain away.

Mangrove trees form swamps as their roots trap mud. These swamps are rich in wildlife.

EARTH ALERT!

To humans, wetlands are wastelands. But to millions of birds, they are home. By draining and building on marshes and swamps, people leave these birds with nowhere to breed, rest and feed.

Waterfalls

Rivers wear away rock to make low areas called valleys. The water cannot cut as deeply into hard rock as soft rock. So where a river crosses from one to the other, a step forms. The water roars over it as a waterfall.

INFORMATION OVERLOAD!

E.T. has collected so many fascinating facts that he must send them back to his planet to be analysed.

There is much less water in the Earth's rivers than in its seas. If the seas emptied, the rivers would take 37,000 years to fill them.

Every hour, the Earth's biggest river, the 6,570 kilometre-long Amazon of South America, carries enough water to the sea for everyone in the world to have a bath!

Just one lake – Russia's Lake Baikal – contains one-fifth of all the fresh (non-salty) water on the Earth.

Forests and Woodlands

Trees are nature's giants. Growing together in forests and woodlands, they help keep the Earth's atmosphere healthy. Trees provide us with materials such as wood, as well as fruits and medicines. Forests are home to more than half the types of plants and animals in the world.

Many forests in cool places are green only in the spring and summer. Trees lose their leaves in the autumn and stop growing in the winter.

Pine forests

Pine trees grow in the world's coldest countries. They have leaves like needles and 'flowers' called cones. The green needles always stay on the trees, so the trees are called evergreens.

PINE TREE

NEEDLES   CONE

EARTH ALERT!

Half of the Earth's great forests have disappeared because we have cut down trees carelessly to get wood for building and paper-making. Unless we start to plant and harvest trees like crops, tropical forests will be gone by 2020.

Some woodlands in cool countries contain a mix of evergreen trees and trees that lose their leaves in the winter.

Rainforests

The steamiest, greenest forests are in the hot, wet regions near the Equator, an imaginary circle around the Earth's middle. They are called tropical rainforests. Rainforests have three main layers – a thick roof of leaves at the top, a middle layer of woody plants, and a ground floor where moss and fungi grow. Rainforest and other trees absorb harmful gases from the air and put back life-giving oxygen.

More plants and animals live in rainforests than anywhere else in the world.

INFORMATION OVERLOAD!

E.T. has collected so many fascinating facts that he must send them back to his planet to be analysed.

Every year, each American uses one whole tree in the form of timber (trimmed wood), paper and other forest products.

Indians who live in South America's rainforests know how to use 1,300 plants as medicines.

In an area of rainforest the size of a sports stadium, there are as many as 42,000 different sorts of insect.

Deserts

Some of the Earth's deserts look so like another planet that E.T. gets homesick. Very little rain falls in these strange places. But by using clever ways to gather and save water, a few types of plant and animal can live in the heat and dryness.

When thirsty camels reach water, they can drink a bathtubful in 10 minutes.

The Sahara is the world's biggest desert. It covers much of North Africa.

PHONE HOME FACTS

The Atacama Desert in Chile, South America, is the driest place on the Earth. Rain falls there only two or three times in every 100 years.

How deserts form

Desert-making begins when the Sun heats moist air at the Equator. The hot, damp air rises, then drops its water as rain. The air is then dry, so the lands it travels over receive little or no rain. This is why most deserts lie on either side of the Equator. There are also some deserts on coasts, where oceans cool and dry the air.

Sand and stones

Deserts are not just giant sandpits. Only one-tenth of the Sahara is made of sand hills called dunes. Much more desert scenery is bare rock, and some of it is covered with stones. This rocky desert landscape is in Libya, North Africa.

Smart plants and animals

There is so little water in deserts that plants and animals have special ways to stay alive. The cactus plants in this North American desert, for example, collect drops of water from the air on their spines. Many small creatures avoid the heat by hiding away in the day, and feeding at night. Other animals, such as camels, can live on small amounts of water, keeping it in their bodies for a long time.

INFORMATION OVERLOAD!

E.T. has collected so many fascinating facts that he must send them back to his planet to be analysed.

The Sahara Desert is almost as big as the whole of the USA. It covers about 8,600,000 square kilometres.

The world's largest sand-only desert is the Great Desert of Libya. The second largest is the Grand Erg (sand sea) of Algeria.

Antarctica and other cold places where little rain falls are also deserts. Sand, rock and cold deserts together cover one-third of the Earth's land surface.

Grasslands

E.T. has been on safari to see lions in the grasslands of Africa. Amazing animals make these grasslands famous, but you will find grass-covered areas on every continent. They are sandwiched between forest and desert.

Different names

Every continent has its own name for grasslands. The African savannah, the Australian outback and the South American pampas are all grasslands. So, too, are the North American prairies and the steppes of Central Asia.

NORTH AMERICAN PRAIRIE

Most grasslands are too dry for trees to grow there. But trees can live on the world's wettest grasslands, the savannah.

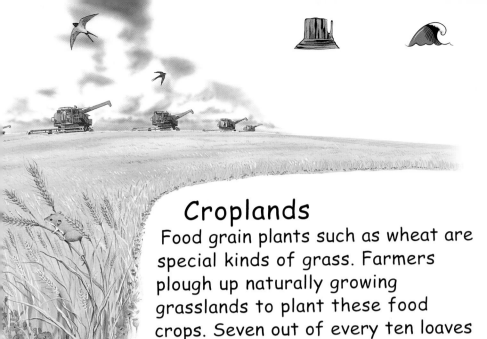

Croplands

Food grain plants such as wheat are special kinds of grass. Farmers plough up naturally growing grasslands to plant these food crops. Seven out of every ten loaves eaten in the USA are made from wheat grown on the prairies.

Why do zebras have stripes?

The savannah is dangerous for zebras and other big, plant-eating animals because lions kill and eat them. Although there is nowhere to hide away from lions, the zebras' striped coats help them to blend in with the grass and they can run very fast.

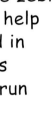

EARTH ALERT!

Twenty-five million bison (wild cattle) once lived on North America's grasslands. European settlers started hunting them in about 1870. In under 15 years, almost all the bison were dead.

INFORMATION OVERLOAD!

E.T. has collected so many fascinating facts that he must send them back to his planet to be analysed.

Humans made some of the Earth's grassland. For example, the Polynesian people of New Zealand created grassland when they burned down forests.

Some of Africa's grassland is turning into desert. This means there is not enough grass to feed all the grass-eating animals there.

Fires started by lightning help some savannah plants. The heat makes the plants drop their seeds. The fire burns weeds so they do not smother the seeds as they grow.

Life on Earth

The Earth is the only place we know where humans exist. But most other animals and plants have been here much longer. Through greed and carelessness, we are killing many of these living things. E.T. thinks that we must start looking after our precious planet.

Light for life

Sunlight keeps everything on the Earth alive. Plants need light to grow, and animals need plants for food. Humans use plants and animals. So without the Sun's light, there would be no life on Earth.

Different kinds of life

Most of the living things that we see around us are plants and animals. Plants grow by using a green chemical in their leaves to make food from sunlight, air and water. Animals feed on plants, or on other animals that eat plants. Unlike plants, animals can move around. They also have senses such as sight and hearing.

Thousands of plants and animals live in rainforests.

Tiny plants and animals called plankton still fill the oceans. They are food for larger creatures such as fish.

Slow change

Life on Earth began over 2,000 million years ago. The first living things were small sea creatures. Constant slow change, called evolution, produced the range of plants and creatures around today. Life on Earth depends on this huge variety.

Planting trees helps to get rid of gases that are warming the Earth. But it will not replace living things that have died out.

Gases from burning coal and oil are warming the Earth's climate. Many plants and animals cannot stand the heat.

The Earth's future

Humans are poisoning the Earth's air and water with factory chemicals. We are also destroying forests, swamps and other places. This often makes the animals and plants that live there die out. Unless people take more care, life on Earth will become impossible.

INFORMATION OVERLOAD!

E.T. has collected so many fascinating facts that he must send them back to his planet to be analysed.

There are probably more than 13 million different kinds of living thing on the Earth. Scientists have described and named only one-eighth of them.

Humans are dangerous. Living things are dying out 1,000 times faster now than before we lived on the Earth.

People discover more than 7,000 new kinds of insect each year. In 2001, a new poisonous spider was found at Windsor Castle, a home of Britain's queen.

GOING HOME

E.T. has found out all he needs to know about Planet Earth and now he is ready to go home. Help him get back to his spaceship.

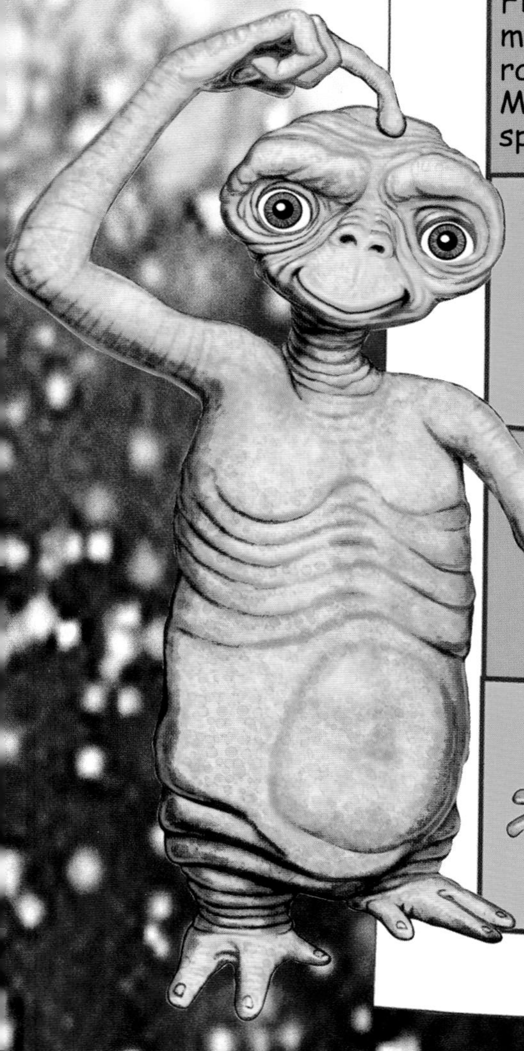

40

41

42 The iceberg you are floating on melts. Go back to 37.

43 Why the Beco the quak

39 Find a new medicine in a rainforest. Move on 1 space.

38 Slide down a slippery glacier to 19.

37

36 Why didn't the stars come to E.T.'s party? Because he didn't planet.

20

21

22

23

19

18

17 Whirling wind blows you up to 21.

16 Wai for

START

1 Reach the summit of Mount Everest. Move on 2 spaces.

2

3 He th th lay on

the dice then move the right number of squares.
...ce you get to the end, blast off home.

45

46

47 Caught using a spray-can full of CFCs. Go back to 32.

Discover life on another planet. Move on 1 space.

BLAST OFF !

Find a **34** fabulous fossil. Move on to 44.

33

32

31 Shaken up by an earthquake Go back to 28.

30

25

Trapped **26** in waterless desert. Go back 2 spaces.

27

28

Shocked **29** by a volcanic eruption. Go down to 10.

Slip down **14** into the Grand Canyon. Go back to 5.

13

12 Dig up a garnet. Move on 4 spaces.

11

10

5 What did the boy volcano say to the girl volcano? I lava you.

6

7

8 Surf a towering tsunami up to 11.

9

Index